Masterpieces
of Italian Violin Making
1620-1850

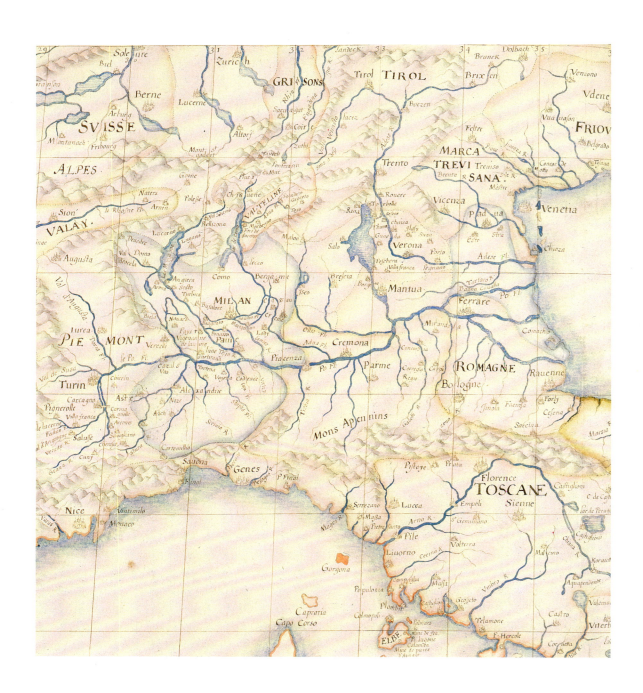

'Carte d'Italie' by an anonymous cartographer, c.1750.
From the King George III collection in the British Library.

MASTERPIECES OF
Italian Violin Making
1620-1850

Twenty-six important stringed instruments from
the Collection at the Royal Academy of Music

DAVID RATTRAY
Photographs by Clarissa Bruce

ROYAL ACADEMY OF MUSIC: LONDON

First published 1991
© David Rattray 1991
© Forewords, Charles Beare, Malcolm Sadler and Peter Biddulph

Produced by Editorial and Production Services Ltd
Printed and bound in Great Britain by
Elwick Grover Aicken for
The Royal Academy of Music
Marylebone Road, London NW1 5HT

ISBN 0 9517271 0 9

Contents

Preface

The co-operation and kindness of many people have made possible the publication of this book.

Thanks are due, first and foremost, to J. & A. Beare, Peter Biddulph, Ealing Strings and Sotheby's of London, whose generosity and enthusiasm for the project have been splendid. I owe Charles Beare and all the staff at J. & A. Beare a debt of gratitude for their help and advice, particularly John Dilworth who, besides his excellent contributions to and editing of the text, suggested the title for the book. Thanks should also go to British Reserve for backing the project.

The quality of the photographs is due to the work and patience of Clarissa Bruce, of the Musical Instrument Department of Sotheby's London, during the year in which the instruments were photographed. The Stradivari cello of 1726 was photographed by courtesy of Sotheby's, New York, kindly arranged by Charles Rudig. The head views of the Amati 1671, Stradivari 1734 and Pressenda 1847 are included by courtesy of J. & A. Beare.

Further thanks to John Maddison and Daphne Terry of Editorial and Production Services Ltd, for the production and editing of the book; to Philippa Kingsbury who supplied the information on Rutson's life, as well as the cameo of Rutson; to all my colleagues at the Academy who contributed to the book, including Peter Shellard, John White, Howard Davis, Christopher Regan and Lisa Shaw; and, finally, to the Board of Directors of the Royal Academy of Music, whose support and enthusiasm for the book have been much appreciated.

David Rattray

6

Foreword by Charles Beare

From the beginning, the best sounding musical instruments of the violin family were made in Italy, and the finest of all in the city of Cremona. In the hundreds of years that have passed since the working life of Andrea Amati of Cremona (c.1505-77), his and his followers' violins, violas and cellos have remained unchallenged, and with the spread of classical music worldwide they have become ever more valuable rarities, the best of them only affordable by the very wealthy.

In the eighteenth and nineteenth centuries British travelling merchants and aristocrats were able to acquire antiquities and works of art in Europe more or less at will, and in consequence many of the best Italian instruments found their way to our shores. During the past hundred years most of them have left again, and it is therefore fortunate that a few have been willed to the collections of our country's music colleges, and in particular that of the Royal Academy of Music, which owns no fewer than six instruments by Antonio Stradivari (1644-1737), the greatest violin maker of all time.

The Academy's instruments were left to them by generous patrons of music, for the benefit of music in this country. Those players who have borrowed them have all testified to the advantage of performing on great instruments – the range of tone colour, the extra resonance, the speedy response to the bow, the depth and carrying power.

Some countries have banks and foundations willing to purchase instruments in support of their national musicians. Others have abundant state collections. In our own there appears to be no government and little institutional help available to young performers who need and deserve the extra help and incentive in their careers that the availability of a great violin, viola or cello can give. The collection illustrated and ably described in this book is, therefore, the greater part of our national pool of fine old instruments, remaining alongside a still substantial number in private hands.

The publication of this book celebrates the fact that these instruments form an exceptional collection, and that their continued use in British music is the correct way to carry out their donors' wishes and to repay their generosity.

Foreword by Malcolm Sadler

The mystery and magic of the violin – its form and its sound – centre mainly on the early Italian master instruments, especially those from Cremona. Later makers have striven, and still strive today, to emulate them; and players search unceasingly for the elusive tonal qualities associated with the period.

In spite of many claims, no one has yet been able to explain fully the successes of those early craftsmen. Obviously, many factors come into consideration and time may also have played a part, although it must be admitted that old non-Italian instruments do not reveal the same attributes. This gives credence to the notion that early Italian luthiers possessed certain secrets. If indeed they did, then those secrets must be hidden somewhere within the pages that follow.

By making their collection of instruments available in catalogue form, the Royal Academy of Music is giving everybody a special opportunity to enjoy some of the truly great creations of the past. Ealing Strings supports the project whole-heartedly and commends the production to all lovers of the violin.

Foreword by Peter Biddulph

The Royal Academy of Music can be justifiably proud of its fine collection of stringed instruments. Which music school, other than the Royal Academy, can boast possession of six instruments by Antonio Stradivari? The publication of this book will highlight the generosity of all those patrons of music who have bequeathed their instruments to the Academy, and keep alive their wish that they should be played.

The Academy has also shown great initiative in adopting a 'Luthier in Residence' to care for the collection, at this time very ably managed by David Rattray. Let us hope that our other music colleges will follow the example of the Academy and appoint their own resident luthier.

The violin maker today has had to adapt his skill to that of conservationist and restorer, and at no other time has that skill been more needed than now. The Royal Academy has set the wheels in motion by giving violin makers the status and recognition they deserve. I for one would be nowhere without their skill – but that is another story.

John Rutson 1829-1906

This book is dedicated to the memory of John Rutson and commemorates the centenary in 1990 of his bequest to the Royal Academy of Music.

Rutson's forebears hailed from the North of England where they were cloth merchants, dyers and weavers. In the eighteenth century they became prominent citizens of Kendal in Cumbria. With further prosperity, William Rutson, John's father, moved in 1832 to Northallerton in the North Riding of Yorkshire where he bought the estates of Newby Wiske and Nunnington Hall (the latter is now owned by the National Trust).

In due course John Rutson inherited both estates, for he was the eldest of three remaining sons, the fourth having died young. Educated at Trinity College, Cambridge, he remained a lifelong bachelor. He was an intelligent and enthusiastic amateur, and was a well-known and generous patron of music. His interests lay in education and the arts, and in acquiring two remarkable collections, one of drawings and watercolours, the other of musical instruments, principally violins. He was a Director of the Royal Academy of Music and a Member of the Council of the Royal College of Music, and assisted many students to pursue their studies at the Academy, often lending or giving them instruments from his collection to help them start their professional careers. The Oslif Rutson Memorial Prize was also instituted by him in 1890, in remembrance of his brother, and is still in existence today. Rutson died on 31 July 1906, aged seventy-seven.

Undoubtedly his most generous bequest was made to the Royal Academy of Music in 1890. This included four instruments by Stradivari – the 'Long Pattern' violin (1694), the 'Archinto' viola (1696), the 'Maurin' violin (1718) and the 'Habeneck' violin (1734), and three instruments by members of the Amati family – a viola by the brothers Antonio and Girolamo (1620) and violins by Nicolo (1662) and Girolamo II (1671). The bequest also included violins by Pressenda (1833), Cappa (c.1690) and Rota (1800).

Rutson will long be remembered, both locally and nationally, for his benefaction to the Academy, which forms the basis of the collection of important stringed instruments that are featured in this book.

Antonio and Girolamo Amati: Cremona Viola 1620

The Amati tradition of violin making in Cremona spans four generations. Andrea Amati (c.1505-1577) who can be called 'the father of violin making', brought the shape of the violin to perfection and generally established the sizes and proportions as they exist today. (Examples of his work can be seen in the Ashmolean Museum, Oxford, the Carlisle Museum, and the Shrine to Music at Vermillion, South Dakota, USA.)

Andrea's two sons were Antonio (b.1540) and Girolamo (1561-1630). Commonly known as 'the Brothers Amati', we know from a document dated 1580 that they inherited their father's business. Eight years later Girolamo bought out his brother's share, although both names continued to appear on the labels.

They developed the craft of violin making, subtly changing the soundholes, edge and purfling, giving their instruments an elegance which has never been surpassed. They also experimented with new outlines and archings which improved the sonority of their instruments.

They were prolific makers, for as well as two sizes of violins (345mm and 352mm) they made large cellos (50mm bigger than modern cellos) and large violas, known as tenors, which had back lengths of up to 457mm, commonly played at the time. These tenors were tuned in the same way as the smaller, contralto viola, but scored for parts with lower registers. The Brothers Amati are also thought to have made the first Cremonese contralto viola in 1615, of dimensions still considered ideal.

The Academy's magnificent viola of 1620 is of particular interest, as it is one of the few surviving tenors which has not been reduced in size for modern playing.

It is worth comparing the outline of this viola with the Brothers' violin of 1629 (see pp. 14, 15). There is much similarity in the lower bouts, while the middle and upper bouts are also similar but elongated. The arching is typically scooped at the edges, but not excessively high, measuring 19mm at the back.

The beautifully formed corners are long, slender and hooked, and the edges have a light and delicate appearance. The purflings are bold and clean, and inlaid with superb precision, while the perfectly formed mitres deflect towards the centre bouts. The Amati purfling is made of poplar, between strips of pear wood dyed jet-black; the beautiful preparation and inlaying of the Brothers' purflings set standards for all violin makers to follow. The elegantly cut soundholes are typical of their work, with the narrow, lower wings relieved by a subtle fluting; equally typical are the upright stance and wide spacing.

The head is well proportioned and possesses flat cheeks in the style of a cello head, although not so excessively wide as to obstruct the player's hand. From the side can be seen the long and elegant pegbox and the sharply cut scroll. The volutes are dished and become increasingly deep from the second turn onwards.

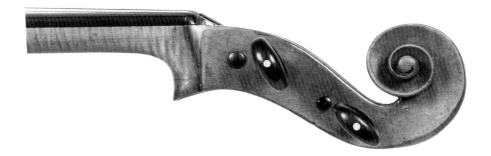

The head is slab cut, as is the case with the Brothers' 1629 violin (see pp. 14, 15). This makes the curl of the wood much more prominent in the back of the pegbox than the sides. This practice of cutting the head on the slab is uncommon with later makers, but is a feature of earlier instruments made in Cremona and Brescia. The two-piece back is of maple with a narrow curl, with similar ribs, and the front is of straight, close-grained pine.

The Amatis covered their instruments in the now legendary golden-brown Cremonese varnish, but as with many instruments of the seventeenth century and before, most of the top coat of varnish, which was originally quite soft, has all but worn away, revealing the warm golden coloured ground coat. The composition of this ground, or wood preparation, was known to violin makers throughout Italy between 1540 and 1760. It served several functions, preserving and protecting the wood, and preventing the colourful top coat from sinking into the pores, thus allowing the figure and grain of the wood to shine through with maximum transparency and reflectiveness.

The powerful sound of the viola is both penetrating and masculine. In 1982 the violist Paul Silverthorne took up the challenge of adapting to the size of the instrument, and having explored and developed its tonal possibilities, the viola became an integral part of his performing. This combination has led to several new works, including compositions by Richard Rodney Bennett, *After Ariadne*; Elizabeth Lutyens, *Echo of the Wind* for solo viola; and Robert Saxton, *Viola Concerto*.

PRINCIPAL DIMENSIONS (mm)

Body			Edge Thickness (back)	
length	451		corners	4.2
upper bouts	214		centre	3.6
middle bouts	149		bouts	3.5
lower bouts	263			
			Stop Length	247
Rib Heights				
neck root	38.5		Modern	
upper corner	39.5		Neck Length	159.5
lower corner	40.5			
end pin	40.5			

Antonio and Girolamo Amati: Cremona

Violin 1629

In 1628 Cremona was devastated by famine and two years later plague swept through the city, killing Girolamo; his elder brother, Antonio, had died some time before. Girolamo's son Nicolo (b.1596), who was his only pupil, was suddenly the only maker of any consequence living in Italy. But for his survival, violin making in Cremona almost certainly would have ended before its greatest days. Amati instruments made between 1620 and 1630 were labelled with the names of the brothers Antonio and Girolamo; but the dominant hand was in fact that of Nicolo Amati.

This violin of 1629 is a rare and beautiful example. The workmanship throughout is sharp and precise, although clinical perfection was not one of the desired characteristics of Cremonese violin making. The sweeping lines of the body flow effortlessly together and the corners are long and pronounced. The arching is of a medium height and full in the flanks.

The elegant and petite soundholes, with their lightly sculpted lower wings, are characteristic of the Amatis, but are more curved and the spacing proportionally closer than in the viola of 1620. The shape of the head and the turns of the scroll, however, anticipate the Nicolo Amati violin of 1662 (see pp. 16, 17). The back is in one piece of slab-cut maple. The ribs are quarter sawn and evenly figured; the bottom rib remains uncut, in one continuous piece across the bottom block. The table is of fine-to-medium-grained spruce. The slab-cut head again shows its most attractive figure when viewed from the front and back.

Like the Brothers' 1620 viola the top coat of varnish has worn away, apart from a few traces, leaving the beautiful ground in full view.

PRINCIPAL DIMENSIONS (mm)

Body			Edge Thickness (back)	
length	355		corners	4
upper bouts	168		centre	3.6
middle bouts	112		bouts	3.5
lower bouts	206			
			Stop Length	194.5
Rib Heights				
neck root	28.4			
upper corner	30			
lower corner	32.5			
end pin	31			

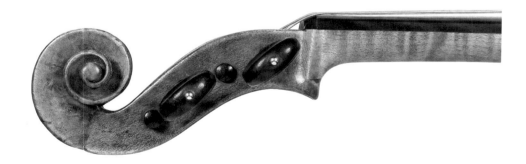

Nicolo Amati: Cremona
Violin 1662

Nicolo Amati (1596-1684), the son of Girolamo, has the reputation of being the most refined craftsman of the family, and is certainly the most highly regarded. He exerted the widest influence of any single maker through his pupils and followers who themselves became well-known makers, the most famous of them all being Antonio Stradivari.

This Amati violin of 1662 is a well-preserved and beautiful example. The model for it was Nicolo's largest and most favoured, known as the 'Grand Amati'; this design was one of his greatest achievements and its dimensions are today considered ideal.

In Amati instruments the curve of the arching is hollowed and rises gently, slightly in from the purfling – a characteristic which is more exaggerated in Nicolo's instruments than in those of his father or grandfather. Although providing the sweet tone in fashion at the time, this arching restricts the vibration in the table. This was later resolved by Stradivari, whose arching rises quickly from the edge, thus acoustically increasing the vibrating area of the plates, and the fullness of tone.

The outline is rounded and flowing, with the corners less elongated than on earlier Amati instruments; the edges have their customary delicate and light appearance. The wide purfling is inlaid with great precision, the long mitres flowing together perfectly. The finely cut soundholes complement the outline and are cut with much flair, in a style beautifully representative of the maker.

The head is also in keeping with the Amati tradition. The scroll is delicately carved, clean and compact, although the back of the pegbox is considerably worn through years of use. The wood is of a plainer cut than that of the back and ribs, which are of an attractive, tightly figured quarter-sawn maple. The pine of the table is very narrow-grained in the middle, becoming wider in the flanks. The remaining original varnish is a honey-brown colour.

PRINCIPAL DIMENSIONS (mm)

Body			*Edge Thickness (back)*	
length	354		corners	3.6
upper bouts	167		centre	3.5
middle bouts	111		bouts	3.25
lower bouts	207			
Rib Heights			*Stop Length*	196
neck root	28.5			
upper corner	29.5			
lowre corner	30			
end pin	30.5			

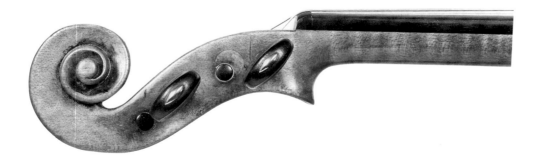

Girolamo Amati II: Cremona

Violin 1671

Girolamo Amati II (1649-1740) was the son of Nicolo Amati, and also the last member of the family to be connected with the craft of violin making. He was a fine craftsman, capable of producing a masterpiece, although his work is often overshadowed by the great achievements of the earlier members of his family. He assisted his ageing father until about 1670, and from then on worked unaided, though continuing to label his instruments 'Nicolo Amati' until his father's death in 1684.

The beautiful violin of 1671 is in keeping with the best traditions of his family. Like much of his output it is modelled on the smaller pattern of Nicolo, which was much favoured in its time for its bright tone and quick response.

The arching is marginally less scooped at the edges than the work of his father, but at the same time Girolamo II's style is slightly stiffer in appearance, particularly in the bouts and around the soundholes, which show a return to the more upright position of earlier work by the Brothers Amati, seen clearly on the 1620 viola (see pp. 10-13). The shaping of the edges and the beautifully inlaid purfling are of a very high standard. The soundholes are well sited, giving the optimum stop length. Looking at the head, the volutes and the channels around the scroll are of a clean and elegant cut, but the scroll itself is less conscientiously symmetrical than the work of his forefathers.

The wood of the table is in one piece of pine with wide grain in the bass moving to tight grain in the treble. Classical makers generally preferred to make their fronts in two matching pieces split from a single wedge, which was then opened out like a book, and glued along the centre.

The back and ribs are of medium-figured maple, the head somewhat plainer. The varnish, which now only partially covers the instrument, is warm brown and slightly opaque. Areas around the middle bouts, where the varnish retains its original consistency, have a fine crazing. The ground is gold-brown coloured.

The Amati can be heard to good effect alongside the Dalla Costa violin (see pp. 54-5) in the recordings of the Bingham Quartet listed in the Discography (p. 71).

PRINCIPAL DIMENSIONS (mm)

Body		Rib Heights		Edge Thickness (back)		Stop Length	195
length	352	neck root	28.5	corners	3.4		
upper bouts	160.5	upper corner	29	centre	3.3		
middle bouts	111	lower corner	30	bouts	3.2		
lower bouts	200	end pin	30.2				

Girolamo Amati II: Cremona
Violin *c*.1713

After 1700 Girolamo Amati II produced relatively few instruments. However, the violin of *c*.1713 is of particular interest. Made when he was about sixty-four, it is an extremely late and handsome example of his work. The modelling is very different from earlier instruments from his father's workshop; it is larger and more rugged in appearance, the arching stronger and rising immediately from the purfling, and somewhat full in the upper and lower flanks. The fluting around the edge is shallow.

The one-piece back is of irregular curl, the ribs quarter sawn of mixed figure, the table is of medium-grained spruce, and marked with broad reed lines. The varnish, although slightly clouded, is an attractive red-brown colour and of fine quality.

All the members of the Amati family and their pupils had, and were probably encouraged to have, a different approach to finishing the purfling – almost as a trademark. Girolamo chose to deflect his purfling mitres quite strongly across the corner.

The head is of a plain-cut maple and is generously proportioned, the second turn of the volute being characteristically wide. Looking at the back of the pegbox and the turns of the volutes one can see unblended tool marks, perhaps an indication of the maker's failing hand.

It must have been clear to all at the time, including Girolamo, that his nearby contemporary Antonio Stradivari was the best and most successful maker in Cremona, and now held the position of eminence once held by the Amati family. Girolamo may have been sufficiently wealthy to be able to stop working, but whatever the reason, as there are no known instruments labelled later than 1713 he would seem to have given up the craft long before his death in 1740.

Academy records show only that the violin was donated by a Miss Kerson.

PRINCIPAL DIMENSIONS (mm)

Body			*Edge Thickness (back)*	
length	354.5		corners	3.9
upper bouts	168		centre	3.4
middle bouts	112		bouts	3
lower bouts	206.5			
Rib Heights			*Stop Length*	195
neck root	30.3			
upper corner	31.3			
lower corner	32.3			
end pin	31.2			

Antonio Stradivari: Cremona
Violin 1694 'Rutson'

The great and prolific violin maker Antonio Stradivari of Cremona (1644-1737) experimented constantly throughout his exceptionally long working life, improving the design of the violin with each subtle development, and setting a standard which has never been surpassed.

He based his early work, from 1666, on that of Nicolo Amati, using it to form his own style during the 1680s. In 1690, aged forty-six, he embarked on his first radical departure in design, when he introduced his 'Long Pattern'.

Looking to the work of the Brescian makers of the previous century, Gasparo da Salo and Maggini, whose instruments carry a reputation for a deep sonority and are often well over the standard length of 355mm established by Amati, Stradivari extended the body length of his violins by up to 12mm. With typical thoroughness, he adjusted all the other proportions to suit, and the violins he produced to this pattern between 1690 and 1700 are the most elegant he ever made.

The Academy collection contains two exceptional examples of the 'Long Pattern' Stradivarius. One is dated 1694, and came into the collection as part of the Rutson bequest.

The arching to some degree is Amati-influenced, being slightly scooped at the edges, but the table arch possesses the characteristic Stradivari flatness in its length, whilst the back arch has a softly rounded curve.

The Amati influence can also be seen in the delicate edgework and the beautiful purflings with their up-turned mitres. The soundholes, too, have the Amati elegance but are slightly longer and the wings broader and squarer. Stradivari's style of sculpting the lower wings more emphatically gives his soundholes an extra dimension. The pegbox is tapered, giving a wide throat beneath the superbly carved and compact scroll.

The back is made in one piece of strikingly figured maple, with matching ribs, with the figure sloping in the opposite direction. The head is marked with a bolder curl. The table is of tight-grained spruce which opens to a medium width in the bouts. Much of the top coat of varnish is worn away, but what remains is similar to that of the 1696 viola 'Archinto' (see pp. 24-7). The ground is not only highly attractive but has demonstrated its wonderful preserving qualities.

PRINCIPAL DIMENSIONS (mm)

Body		*Rib Heights*	
length	358	neck root	28.8
upper bouts	161.5	upper corner	29.5
middle bouts	112	lower corner	30
lower bouts	200.5	end pin	30

23

Antonio Stradivari: Cremona

Viola 1696 'Archinto'

During Stradivari's long and productive lifetime he made relatively few violas: only ten complete instruments still exist. For elegance and grandeur, and in view of its remarkable state of preservation, the 'Archinto' of 1696 is arguably the best example known.

Its long and slender corners, delicate edges and precise purfling show the master still looking to the work of Nicolo Amati for inspiration. However, the relationship between the upper and lower bouts and the roundness of the shoulders have much in common with the 'Long Pattern' violins of the 1690s.

The cut of the soundholes is particularly striking; they are modestly proportioned and sit well on the fine-grained belly wood. The lower parts of the soundholes are delightfully accentuated by the straight and well-defined sculpting of the lower wing. The purflings are beautifully flowing and of an even thickness, with extremely long and perfectly formed mitres. The delicate fluting is met with a crisp edge chamfer which still remains sharp and clear.

Looking from the sides the ribs seem relatively low, giving a shallow appearance to the viola. However, Stradivari compensates for this by raising the arching, at the same time giving it greater fullness, resulting in a beautifully rounded form. When the instrument was examined by Count Cozio di Salibue (1755–1840), violin collector and expert and author of *Il Carteggio* (his memoirs of the nineteenth-century violin trade), his opinion was that the unusual lowness of the ribs may have had a restricting effect on the tone. However, those fortunate enough to have heard the instrument agree that it has a warm, sonorous and penetrating sound.

In common with most Stradivari violas the head has been fashioned with a cello-type pegbox which holds both practical and generous dimensions. From the side are revealed the perfectly rounded turns of the scroll, carved with superb precision, the volutes progressively deepening from the first turns through towards the eyes. Looked at from the front, the head appears symmetrical and harmonious. The flutings around the back of the pegbox are almost semicircular in cross section but, as the channels approach the front, they become characteristically flat at the bottom with steep sides, while the central spine continues unwavering to the extreme limit of the throat. The markings of the wood are revealed in a different aspect in this quarter-sawn head, contrasting with the Brothers Amati viola (see pp. 10-13)

The one-piece back is dramatically figured quartered maple. The ribs are from the same log and the figure is slightly tighter. The bottom ribs remain uncut, formed in one long piece – as was the practice of most Cremonese makers. The head wood is of a less pronounced figure, and the front is of an exceptionally tight and narrow-grained spruce.

The varnish is breathtaking, and nearly all the highly transparent top coat remains intact. Light is reflected in an astonishing manner, displaying the superb dichroic qualities of Stradivari's varnish. The colour alters from bright gold-yellow to deep orange and red-brown as the eye moves across the

24

surface. At areas of the back where wear has occurred a highly refractive gold-coloured ground is revealed.

The viola was sold in about 1800 by Count Carlo Gambara of Brescia to Count Archinto of Milan who, in addition, owned a Stradivari cello of 1689 and two violins. The instruments were all purchased by J.B. Vuillaume in about 1860. The viola subsequently came to England where it was acquired by Rutson.

Among the violists to have played the 'Archinto' are Watson Forbes who used it for many years in the Aeolian Quartet, and later his former student Roger Bigley of the Lindsay Quartet.

In 1987 the 'Archinto', along with the 'Habeneck' violin of 1734, was taken back to Cremona for the exhibition marking the 250th anniversary of Stradivari's death.

PRINCIPAL DIMENSIONS (mm)

Body			*Edge Thickness (back)*	
length	416		corners	5.5
upper bouts	185.5		centre	5
middle bouts	130		bouts	4.8
lower bouts	241			
			Stop Length	225
Rib Heights				
neck root	32			
upper corner	33.6			
lower corner	34.1			
end pin	34.5			

Antonio Stradivari: Cremona
Violin 1699 'Kustendyke'

This well-preserved 'Long Pattern' example dated 1699 differs from the violin of 1694 (see pp. 22-3) in several ways. The 'Kustendyke' represents the ultimate development of the 'Long Pattern', but shows signs of the more powerful designs to come. It is even longer in the body and is more rounded in the upper and lower bouts. Its arching is fuller, the curve beginning closer to the purfling.

Other subtle but significant differences include the bolder cut of the soundholes with their deeper sculpted lower wings. The spacing of the soundholes is wider and the scroll broader. The edgework, along with the long corners and fine-grained belly wood, brings to mind the 'Archinto' viola (see pp. 24-7), made three years earlier. The back is in two pieces of figured maple and the instrument retains much of its original deep red-brown varnish.

By 1700 Stradivari had abandoned the 'Long Pattern', and reverted to a 355mm body length, but with increased width and a stronger, more masculine character. Today the 355mm length is the accepted standard, and modern players can find some difficulty adapting to the 'Long Pattern' violins. Their fine tone, however, is ample reward to those who succeed.

The 'Kustendyke' takes its name from a previous Dutch owner. It was sold in the 1920s to Mrs Agnes Scott of Dublin, for just over £1,000, and was left to the Academy in 1961, for the use of Colin Sauer. He has used the violin to record many recitals for the BBC over the years.

PRINCIPAL DIMENSIONS (mm)

Body		*Rib Heights*	
length	362	neck root	29
upper bouts	161	upper corner	30.7
middle bouts	111.5	lower corner	31.2
lower bouts	201	end pin	30.5
Stop Length	197		

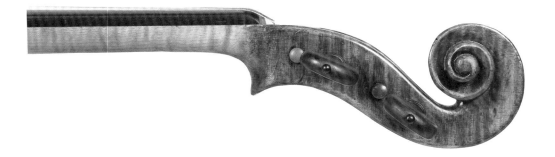

Antonio Stradivari: Cremona
Violin 1718 'Maurin'

The years 1700-18 are widely known as Stradivari's 'golden' period, when he was at the height of his powers as a maker and innovator. The broader, squarer look to his instruments represents a profound move away from the Amati style. By 1710-15 he had taken the tonal and visual aspects of the violin to their zenith, combining strength with elegance, using the finest materials, often dramatically figured maple, and covering his instruments with his transparent and iridescent varnish.

The 'Maurin' of 1718 is an important example of this period. Its shallow and acoustically powerful arching rises to a height of 14.5mm at the back, while the table is slightly higher, with a typical flatness in its length. The edgework is elegant and still reminiscent of the feminine-looking pre-1700 violins, accentuated by the delicate and beautifully inlaid purfling. The points of the corners are filled in with mastic, a feature noticeable in many of Stradivari's later instruments.

The exquisitely cut soundholes are set upright in the body, the treble soundhole leaning fractionally outwards, making the spacing of the upper circles slightly wider than normal (44mm apart), also characteristic of Stradivari's work during this period.

The lower wings are beautifully sculpted, putting the soundholes into sharp relief. The head is compact, refined and superbly balanced; viewed from the back it has a typically generous width to the pegbox opposite the throat. The back is made up of two quarter-sawn wedges of spectacularly figured imported maple, with ribs of a similar cut. The head has a wider flame, and the belly is of fine-grained spruce. The radiant golden ground reflects the light, drawing the full beauty from the fine wood.

The violin takes its name from the celebrated French violinist, Jean Pierre Maurin (1822-94), who studied under Baillot and later with Habeneck (see p. 36) at the Paris Conservatoire, where he succeeded Alard as professor of violin.

This violin has been used by David Martin, and later, by Peter Cropper of the Lindsay Quartet, and can be heard alongside the 'Archinto' viola on numerous recordings made by the Quartet.

PRINCIPAL DIMENSIONS (mm)

Body		Rib Heights		Edge Thickness (back)		Stop Length	193
length	355.5	neck root	29.7	corners	4.5		
upper bouts	167.5	upper corner	31.2	centre	4		
middle bouts	113	lower corner	32	bouts	3.8		
lower bouts	206.5	end pin	31.2				

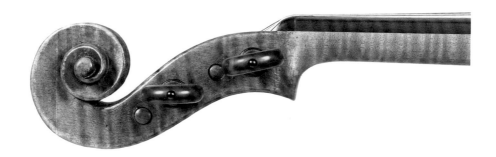

Antonio Stradivari: Cremona

Cello 1726 'Marquis de Corberon'

Before about 1660 the cello was chiefly used as a bass instrument in church music. As the potential of the cello as a solo instrument became apparent and interest grew in the developing repertoire, a new and smaller form of instrument began to evolve. Cremonese makers such as Andrea Guarneri, Francesco Rugeri and Giovanni Battista Rogeri were among the first to design and make cellos of smaller proportions, although some early Brescian cellos are also small.

Stradivari's first period of cello making, from 1680, was taken up with the larger bass, until 1707 when he produced one of his greatest innovations, the design he called the 'Forma B' (*Buona*), which is now generally regarded as the ideal pattern for the cello.

This splendid instrument from 1726 is one of the last known instruments Stradivari made in the B Model. Made when he was 82, it shows the master working in a less refined but still vigorous style. The modelling of the back and belly is full, the arching rising quickly from the edge, and there is a pronounced squareness to the outline, particularly in the C bouts.

The flow and cut of the soundholes, and the carefully inlaid purfling, demonstrate his unwavering knife-control. The carving of the head is clean and precise, but unusually a series of tiny pin holes remains, which were there originally to guide the cutting of the volutes.

It is generally assumed that Stradivari would have been assisted at this time by his two sons, Francesco and Omobono. Their help would have been much needed in view of the great physical effort involved in the carving of a cello back.

Around the early part of the eighteenth century in Cremona, and also throughout Europe, demand seems to have moved towards more hastily made and inexpensive instruments, and possibly even the Stradivari family were feeling the financial effects of this trend.

Economy may therefore have been a factor in the choice of willow for the back and sides of this cello. Because willow is softer, some wear to the back edges has occurred, and the harder woods of the purfling now stand slightly above the surface of the plate. There is also a tonal consideration in the use of willow or poplar, which seems to give cellos a distinctive warmth. However, willow may have been used simply because it eased the task of carving. The head is made from beech, which was very occasionally used by Stradivari and other classical makers as an alternative to maple: the plain character of beech works visually well with the willow. The table wood is wide-grain spruce marked with pronounced reed lines. Even the plainer cuts of wood are given greater appeal under Stradivari's unique and beautiful varnish, and most of the original top coat remains, thickly covering the instrument. The colour is a lush dark orange-brown.

The 'Marquis de Corberon' was presented to the Academy by Audrey Melville in 1960, on the condition that the well-known American cellist Zara Nelsova could have life-long use of the instrument. Miss Nelsova uses the cello in her teaching at the Juilliard School in New York and in her many concert appearances. It has also been heard at the Academy where she has given master classes.

PRINCIPAL DIMENSIONS (mm)

Body		Rib Heights		Edge Thickness (back)			
length	760	neck root	117	corners	5.5	Stop Length	405
upper bouts	343	upper corner	118	centre	5.2	*Modern*	
middle bouts	236	lower corner	118	bouts	4.5	*Neck Length*	280
lower bouts	435	end pin	120				

33

Antonio Stradivari: Cremona
Violin 1734 'Habeneck'

This violin of 1734 is remarkable for its fine state of preservation, and also for the clean, meticulous workmanship of the master in his ninety-first year. It is thought to have been one of the violins still in Stradivari's possession at the time of his death. For the latter part of Stradivari's life he was assisted by his two sons, and certain features of the 'Habeneck', including the cut of the soundholes, would suggest the collaboration of his eldest son Francesco, who was himself sixty-three years of age at the time.

One is immediately struck by the bold, broad outline, with a pronounced squareness to the middle bouts, and the wide corners measuring 7.5mm across. Perfect symmetry was not a priority with Cremonese makers, and obvious differences can be seen in the outline, particularly the middle bouts, but this does not detract from the overall harmony. The edge overhang is also wider than usual for Stradivari violins, giving a slightly long body.

The powerful arching rises immediately from the deep edge fluting, and is particularly full in the flanks. The arching measures 17.5mm at its highest point at the back.

The delicate purflings are artistically inlaid, set relatively far in from the edge with short and tidy mitres pointing straight to the middle of the corner.

The soundholes are each different in shape and character, the top circles large in relation to the bottom ones, and the lower wings distinctly pointed. The top of the treble 'f' is 4mm lower than its neighbour, a discrepancy which, although in this instrument extreme, is quite a common feature of Stradivari's work.

The head is beautifully cut and well proportioned, with a pegbox of a generous width. The volutes are deeply cut from the first turn to the last. The fluting channels at the back of the pegbox are deep and semicircular in shape. The cheeks are marked with tiny vein-like scratches, possibly the result of a rough-edged scraper. The deep swing of the last turn under the eye is a common feature of late Stradivari instruments, and may indicate his son Francesco's handwork. The ink-blackened edge of the chamfer – another consistent feature of Stradivari's work – still partially remains.

The back is in one piece, cut on the slab, with an attractive figure. The ribs are of quarter-sawn maple and the head is of a plainer cut. The varnish which thickly covers most of the instrument is an orange-brown, on top of a warm golden ground which sparkles most beautifully through the top coat.

The violin takes its name from its one-time owner, François-Antoine Habeneck (1781-1849), French virtuoso violinist, conductor and composer. He studied in Baillot's class at the Paris Conservatoire, where he later became a famous professor, and among his pupils were Alard, Léonard, Maurin (see p. 30) and Sainton. The violin was later acquired by the English collector Andrew Fountaine, after whose death in 1872 it passed to John Rutson. The instrument has been

used in the past by players such as Frederick Grinke and Ralph Holmes. Christopher Warren-Green, leader of the London Chamber Orchestra, was lent the violin in 1987.

PRINCIPAL DIMENSIONS (mm)

Body			*Edge Thickness (back)*	
length	358.5		corners	4.5
upper bouts	168		centre	4.1
middle bouts	112		bouts	3.8
lower bouts	207			
			Stop Length	197
Rib Heights				
neck root	29.5			
upper corner	31.1			
lower corner	30.5			
end pin	31			

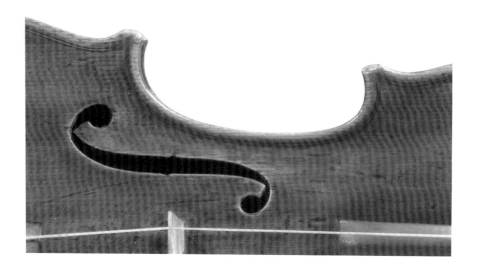

A letter authenticating the provenance of the 'Habeneck' signed by William E. Hill.

38

Giovanni Rota: Cremona
Violin 1800

Giovanni Rota worked in Cremona, *c.*1790-1810, where he was determined to re-establish the standards of violin making which had dipped alarmingly after the death of Stradivari.

This fine violin labelled 1800 is modelled loosely in the style of Stradivari, but the arching is fuller and rather pinched, measuring 20mm in the table. The middle bouts are notably short, and the upper bouts enlarged. The instrument has many attributes, including its fine ground and dark red varnish, though the craftsmanship is less graceful and of a freer nature than the delicate work of his Cremonese predecessors.

Care has been taken over the edge detail, which is of an even thickness around the upper and lower bouts, increasing at the corners. The somewhat pointed button has two deep knife cuts extending from the chamfer, and the soundholes have been sculpted neatly to blend in to the fluting around the edge. The side view reveals a slightly squat pegbox with a widely proportioned scroll looking rather cramped above it. Rota's choice of wood for the back is unusual, in the sense that the grain travels diagonally across the instrument, whilst the front is of good quality medium-width pine, conventionally cut. The thin linings inside the instrument are of dark mahogany, an interesting departure from the more usual choice of willow or pine.

The violin's tone is strong and vibrant and has a good carrying power.

PRINCIPAL DIMENSIONS (mm)

Body			*Edge Thickness (back)*	
length	357		corners	4.6
upper bouts	167		centre	4.4
middle bouts	115		bouts	4.2
lower bouts	208			
			Stop Length	196.5
Rib Heights				
neck root	29			
upper corner	30			
lower corner	31			
end pin	30.5			

Enrico Ceruti: Cremona
Violin 1846

The Ceruti family of violin makers was active in Cremona from the beginning of the nineteenth century. Giovanni Battista Ceruti (*c*.1755-*c*.1817) was a gifted and prolific maker, pupil and successor of the Cremonese maker Lorenzo Storioni. Giovanni's son Joseph (*c*.1787-1860) was an equally good maker but produced relatively few instruments.

Joseph's son Enrico (1808-93) was a musician, holding the position of bass player with the city orchestra as well as being a productive maker. Like that of his forefathers, his workmanship is refined and his style strongly individual. His last known instrument is dated 1881.

This violin, made by Enrico in 1846, is a beautifully preserved example. It shows to good effect the maker's distinctive model with its long and narrow waist, which to some extent necessitates a slightly low position for the soundholes. The arching is Stradivari-influenced, while the fluting above the purfling channel is deep and worked close to the edge of the plates. The soundholes are strikingly bold, and sharply cut with large circles and wide nicks, characteristic of the maker.

The back is in one piece of lightly figured maple, with ribs of a similar cut, the two bottom ribs in one continuous piece. The head is of plain maple, and the table is of two matched pieces of medium-grained pine.

The varnish lacks the earlier Cremonese quality, but is an attractive, transparent, yellow-orange on a pale ground.

PRINCIPAL DIMENSIONS (mm)

Body			Edge Thickness (back)	
length	357		corners	4.2
upper bouts	164		centre	4
middle bouts	107.5		bouts	3.8
lower bouts	205			
			Stop Length	201
Rib Heights				
neck root	30			
upper corner	32			
lower corner	32			
end pin	31.5			

Giovanni Grancino: Milan
Viola *c.*1690

This particularly rare and beautiful viola is an extremely well preserved work of Giovanni Grancino of Milan. Little is known about Grancino, except that he began his career with his brother Francesco about 1670, but he worked alone for most of his life, and his latest known work is dated 1726. He was the earliest and most influential, as well as being one of the best, violin makers of Milan.

The viola has survived the years in remarkable condition, retaining almost all of its highly transparent pale orange varnish. Grancino's style and craftsmanship are seen to good effect in the scroll, which is carved on a bold scale, relieved by the deep and regular cutting of the turns, and in the elegant taper of the pegbox, which has cello-like shoulders. The soundholes are also beautifully cut and show the influence of his Cremonese contemporary, Nicolo Amati, in the graceful swing of both the body and the soundholes; but the wide square wings anticipate the style of Stradivari. The extremely flat curves of the outline into the corners, compared with the deep swing of the outline into the corners seen in Amati work, are also very characteristic of Grancino, and produce short but elegantly drooping top corners.

The purfling, however, is most unusual, and shows Grancino looking towards nearby Brescia for inspiration, where Gasparo Da Salo and Maggini had commonly used double rows of inlay on the magnificent violins and violas they made before 1632. It is an extravagance in which Grancino did not often indulge; indeed many of his later instruments have no purfling at all on the back, merely scratched and painted lines.

The powerful sound of this viola is both warm and penetrating, and can be heard on early recordings by the Alberni Quartet, where it is played by John White. The Grancino passed to his former pupil, Martin Outram, who has used it to record with the Maggini Quartet, and in his own teaching at the Academy. The instrument was played by Bernard Shore in the 1930s, when he was principal viola in the BBC Symphony Orchestra. David Stobbart used it from 1956 to 1963 in several major London orchestras.

PRINCIPAL DIMENSIONS (mm)

Body		Rib Heights		Edge Thickness (back)		Stop Length	226
length	417	neck root	39	corners	4.5		
upper bouts	190	upper corner	38.7	centre	4.4	*Modern*	
middle bouts	133	lower corner	38.7	bouts	3.8	*Neck Length*	142
lower bouts	239	end pin	39.5				

Carlo Antonio Testore: Milan
Violin 1741

The industrious Testore family of violin makers worked in Milan between 1690 and 1760. The Testores, and many of their contemporaries in Naples and Milan during the eighteenth century, were highly productive makers, catering for less wealthy working musicians, rather than the aristocracy or the Church. The declining wealth of the Church, which had hitherto provided instrument makers with the bulk of their patronage, and also the fine supply of Cremonese instruments already in existence, contributed to changing standards.

Carlo Giuseppe Testore was a pupil of Grancino, and their work is often difficult to distinguish. His son Carlo Antonio worked in a similar style, and was capable of fine work as this violin of 1741 demonstrates, but he often slipped to a less refined manner. More often than not his instruments have painted imitation purfling, and he left the back of the pegbox flat, rather than giving it the usual flutings. His brother, Paolo Antonio, and his son, Pietro Antonio, worked successively in cruder styles.

This handsome example, labelled 1741, is in remarkably fresh condition, and has an unbroken covering of thin golden-yellow varnish.

The edgework shows similarity to the Grancino viola (pp. 44-5) in that there is no hollow around the edge following the purfling as is the style of classical instruments. The arching is deeply scooped, rising steeply some distance in from the edge of the plates.

The inlaid purflings consist of a wide central strip between extremely thin blacks. The carving of the scroll is very shallow at the volutes and flutings. The form of the soundholes shows strong similarity to the work of Grancino.

The two-piece back and ribs are of lightly figured maple, and the head is plain. The table is of broad-grain pine, opening to medium in the flanks.

PRINCIPAL DIMENSIONS (mm)

Body		Rib Heights	
length	351	neck root	29.4
upper bouts	165	upper corner	30
middle bouts	108.5	lower corner	30.8
lower bouts	203	end pin	31.2
Stop Length	191		

Carlo Ferdinando Landolfi: Milan
Viola c.1760

Carlo Ferdinando Landolfi worked in Milan c.1750-75, and he is counted among the city's finest makers. It is believed that he may have started as a pupil of the Testores; however, the refinement and style of his work suggest an association with Giovanni Battista Guadagnini, who worked in Milan between 1749 and 1758. Landolfi's pupils include his own son, Pietro Antonio, and Pietro Giovanni Mantegazza.

Landolfi's output was very varied: his instruments include violins and cellos which are slightly undersized according to modern ideals, and also three sizes of viola, measuring between 38.1mm and 40.6mm. This viola made around 1760 is of small dimensions but produces a surprisingly large and even tone.

The squareness of the outline appears rather forceful in comparison with the elegance of some of his other work. Landolfi may have been attempting to enlarge the area of the plates without increasing the body length.

The arching has the fullness found in Guadagnini's instruments, but the edge fluting is deeper and more pronounced. The purfling is neatly inlaid with well-formed mitres. The soundholes are long, narrow, and beautifully cut, still reminiscent of the Amatis.

Unlike those of the other violas featured in this book, the head is violin-styled and shoulderless, the form preferred by players who find the cello type of head restricting to the left hand. The wide second turn of the scroll is a characteristic of the maker, but tends to create a bulky appearance. The varnish is similar in texture to that of the other Milanese instruments described here.

The one-piece back shows a fairly broad figure in the upper bouts, which is deeper in the ribs and head. The belly is of a fine-to-medium-grain spruce.

PRINCIPAL DIMENSIONS (mm)

Body			Rib Heights	
length	385		neck root	34.5
upper bouts	183		upper corner	36
middle bouts	125		lower corner	37
lower bouts	231		end pin	36.5
Stop Length	207			

Giovanni Battista Guadagnini: Milan Violin *c.*1753

The Guadagnini family of violin makers worked from the 1730s until the beginning of the twentieth century. Giovanni Battista is regarded as the finest craftsman in the family, as well as being the most important and original Italian maker of the mid to late eighteenth century. He was a highly prolific maker and also a much travelled man, living and working in no less than five different towns around Italy. He spent his early years in Piacenza assisting his father Lorenzo, who was the first known maker in the family. By the late 1730s Giovanni Battista Guadagnini was working alone, improving his instruments both acoustically and aesthetically. Today, his instruments are much sought after by concert violinists for their brilliant tone and carrying power.

The violin of 1753 is from his Milan period. The modelling is much influenced by violins of Stradivari's late period, having a strong and masculine outline, with particularly bold corners. The arching is high without being unduly bulbous and the purfling is smoothly inlaid, the white centre typically made from walnut, and with particularly thin black strips.

The unique design and cut of the soundholes, with their elongated lower circles, and the long and tapering wings, are a feature of Guadagnini's work. The head is not quite symmetrical but is cut with great verve and flow. The two-piece maple back has a wide curl, ascending from the joint, and the ribs and head are of a plainer cut. The table is of fine-grain pine, broadening slightly towards the flanks. The varnish is dark orange-red, over a golden ground.

This Guadagnini was left to the Academy by the Hungarian violinist Ludwig Straus (1835-99), who studied at the Conservatoire in Vienna from 1842-44 under Hellmesberger and later with Bohm until 1850. He made a successful début as a soloist in 1853. In 1864 he arrived in London and in the following year was appointed leader at the Philharmonic Society, and also became a professor of violin at the Royal Academy of Music. In 1888 he settled in Manchester where he led the Hallé Orchestra.

PRINCIPAL DIMENSIONS (mm)

Body			*Edge Thickness (back)*	
length	355		corners	3.1
upper bouts	167		centre	3.4
middle bouts	113.5		bouts	3.6
lowr bouts	204			
			Stop Length	192
Rib Heights				
neck root	29.5			
upper corner	30.6			
lower corner	31.8			
end pin	32.7			

Giovanni Battista Guadagnini: Parma Violin *c.*1765

Guadagnini worked in Parma between 1759 and 1771, and this violin is dated *c.*1765. The workmanship throughout is clean and sharp, the modelling again is in the maker's bold and individual style, and the arching is influenced by Stradivari, being particularly full in the table. The edge fluting is shallow around the purfling channel, and the corners characteristically decrease in thickness as they approach their extremes. The carefully inlaid purflings are broad and fairly even in thickness: the walnut grain in the white centre strip is clearly visible.

A feature of the Parma and later Turin periods are the soundholes, in which the nicks are positioned well below mid-point, giving a slightly low bridge position. The head is impressive, and from the side can be seen the sweeping curves of the pegbox and extremely high cut throat. The scroll is well proportioned, and finished with a broad chamfer. The one-piece slab-cut back is of a horizontal narrow curl, the contrasting ribs are quarter sawn and of a medium figure, and the head is almost plain. The fine varnish is rich orange-brown.

The violin was left to the Academy by Winifred Small, who died in 1979. A professor at the Academy from 1941-71, she was one of the most successful students of Rowsby Woof and made her Wigmore Hall début when she was still in her teens. The violin produces a massive sound which is both dark and penetrating.

PRINCIPAL DIMENSIONS (mm)

Body			*Edge Thickness (back)*	
length	355		corners	2.9
upper bouts	167		centre	3.2
middle bouts	111.5		bouts	3
lower bouts	205			
			Stop Length	196.5
Rib Heights				
neck root	29.9			
upper corner	30.5			
lower corner	30.7			
end pin	31.4			

Pietro Antonio Dalla Costa: Treviso Violin *c.*1762

Dalla Costa worked principally in Treviso *c.*1740-68, and is classified with the Venetian school of violin makers. He is a comparatively little known maker, but one of his violins was owned and played by Mozart.

The Academy's Dalla Costa is a fine example. On the one hand it is typically Venetian in construction and finish, but on the other the outline and the large, freely cut head reflect something of the work of the great Cremonese maker Giuseppe Guarneri 'Del Gesú' (1698-1744).

The violin has much charm and is tonally very effective. However, the craftmanship is rather undisciplined, with an uneven overhang, imprecise purflings and rather tentative edge fluting.

The soundholes are sharply cut, very long and with a vertical stance, but are sited high in the body, producing a slightly short stop length.

The cut of the head gives much openness to the throat, while the volutes are wide, undished and shallow. From the front the scroll appears narrow and the turns are slightly undercut.

Much of the appeal of the violin lies in the beautiful varnish which partially covers the instrument, and is not dissimilar to that used by the Cremonese. However, it has the cracked texture and deep red-brown coloration that distinguish the Venetian recipe.

This violin was the only possession that the violinist Ilse Joseph was able to bring with her from war-torn Germany in 1940, and in the ensuing years Mrs Joseph travelled the world, giving recitals and lectures promoting reconciliation and peace between nations. In 1979 she presented it to the Academy.

PRINCIPAL DIMENSIONS (mm)

Body			*Edge Thickness (back)*	
length	353		corners	3.2
upper bouts	162		centre	3.5
middle bouts	106.5		bouts	3.2
lower bouts	203			
			Stop Length	191
Rib Heights				
neck root	27.3			
upper corner	28			
lower corner	29			
end pin	29.6			

Nicolo Gagliano: Naples
Violin 1735

The Gagliano family of violin makers worked in Naples from about 1700 to the middle of the nineteenth century. Nicolo learned his craft from his father, Alessandro, the first known Neapolitan violin maker. Along with those of his brother Gennaro, Nicolo's instruments are the most sought after, for his work is of a consistently high quality. Like the other members of his family he was a prolific maker.

This violin of 1735, made two years before the death of Stradivari, is an extremely early and beautiful work. The outline, with its long and shallow middle bouts coupled with wide and square lower bouts, is a hallmark of the work of the Gagliano family. The arching on both plates is high, measuring 19.5mm in the table. The widely spaced soundholes have large upper circles which create a slightly top-heavy look. The pegbox is elegantly tapered, the scroll compact and dished from the bottom of the first turn. From the back the squareness of the bottom of the pegbox complements the shape of the bouts.

The two-piece maple back is of a medium curl ascending from the joint; the ribs and slab-cut head are of a similar figure. Nicolo's varnish is orange-brown and reminiscent of the beautiful varnishes covering his father's instruments. Nicolo was the last Gagliano to use this varnish, and indeed he himself abandoned it during his career, as shown by the violin of 1755 (p.58).

PRINCIPAL DIMENSIONS (mm)

Body			Edge Thickness (back)	
length	354		corners	3.2
upper bouts	169.5		centre	3.2
middle bouts	115		bouts	3
lower bouts	214			
			Stop Length	194
Rib Heights				
neck root	28.4			
upper corner	38.8			
lower corner	31.2			
end pin	30.5			

Nicolo Gagliano: Naples
Violin 1755

This violin of 1755 has been modelled much in the style of Stradivari, and has a strong, flat arch. The outline is broad across the middle, quite flat and characteristically square in the C bouts. As with Nicolo's instrument of 1735, it is carefully purfled, and the inlay appears to be made up from beech while the black strips are of a fibrous material which has expanded, slightly cracking the varnish around the shallow flutings. This is a consistent characteristic of the work of the Gagliano family.

The head is of bold proportions – 45mm across the eyes – and the cheeks of the pegbox possess a generous thickness. From the side one can see the attractive curves of the pegbox with its cleanly finished throat. The neatly rounded volutes are deeply hollowed.

The wood is varied in character, the attractive back is slab cut in two pieces, the contrasting ribs are of quarter-sawn figured maple. The wood of the head has a freckled appearance, a locally grown maple frequently used by Neapolitan makers. The yellow varnish covering the instrument is functional but less appealing than that of the 1735 violin. It is harder, and the application thinner, and possibly an alcohol rather than oil-based recipe.

Over the years, the instrument has been of great benefit to many students, who have found the tone warm and penetrating. Academy records show only that the instrument was donated by a Miss Marten.

PRINCIPAL DIMENSIONS (mm)

Body

length	352	
upper bouts	165	
middle bouts	116	
lower bouts	206	

Rib Heights

neck root	29
upper corner	31.5
lower corner	32
end pin	31

Edge Thickness (back)

corners	3.6
centre	3.4
bouts	3.1

Stop Length 193

Joseph Gagliano: Naples
Violin *c*.1780

Joseph Gagliano was the son of Nicolo, and his instruments date from around 1770-1800. Joseph was a fine craftsman, though his later instruments are coarser, reflecting the sense of urgency that the demands of the time placed upon makers. However, the outline of this violin of *c*.1780 still derives its flowing curves from the Gagliano tradition.

The back arch is deeply scooped, but the front arch is full and rises immediately from the purfling, with only a slight fluting around the edge of the plates. The soundholes are of a bold and open cut, positioned with a slight backward slant. The head appears hastily cut, but holds a certain charm. The scroll is characteristically wide for its diameter, in this case ending half a turn less than the traditional volute.

Although the back and sides are of a plain cut of an indigenous type of maple, they look splendid. The head is unfigured and possibly made of fruit wood. The front is of a good quality spruce of medium growth. In areas where the top coat remains intact the varnish is deep orange-brown, transparent and reflective.

Although the instrument is lacking in elegance, it is robust and has good acoustic qualties. It has a warm, rounded tone, although its carrying powers are slightly limited. It makes a fine chamber instrument and has been used frequently with Academy groups.

Academy records state only that the instrument was donated by a Mrs Cheetham.

PRINCIPAL DIMENSIONS (mm)

Body

length	357		
upper bouts	167.5		
middle bouts	114		
lower bouts	205		

Edge Thickness (back)

corners	2.7
centre	3
bouts	3.2

Rib Heights

neck root	29.5
upper corner	30
lower corner	30.5
end pin	30.5

Stop Length 194

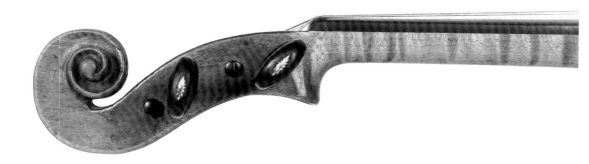

61

Giofredo Cappa: Turin
Violin *c*.1690

Born in the village of Saluzzo near Turin, Giofredo Cappa was one of the city's first and most successful violin makers, receiving patronage from the Prince of Piedmont. It is most likely that he was a pupil of Henricus Catenar, a little-known maker who worked in Turin some years before.

Victorian writers suggested that Cappa may have received training from the Amatis. The general modelling, outline and arching would support this claim – indeed some of his better instruments have been mistaken for those of the Amatis. However, his style was more robust and his method of construction different in several aspects. On the Academy instrument, which is a handsome example, the differences are perceptible in the rather high set, outwardly pointed top corners, clearly visible tool marks particularly around the head and throat, slightly crude purfling made from beech, and soundholes positioned rather low in the body.

Nevertheless, his fine gold-brown varnish compares favourably with the best Cremonese finishes of the time, and the tone is full bodied, sweet and penetrating.

PRINCIPAL DIMENSIONS (mm)

Body			*Edge Thickness (back)*	
length	352		corners	4.5
upper bouts	167		centre	3.6
middle bouts	107		bouts	3.9
lower bouts	205			
			Stop Length	196
Rib Heights				
neck root	28			
upper corner	30			
lower corner	30			
end pin	30.2			

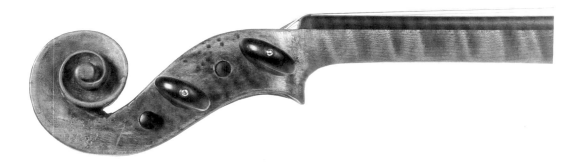

Giovanni Francesco Celoniato: Turin
Cello 1740

Celoniato worked in Turin *c*.1720-40, he and Spirito Sorsano being pupils of Cappa.

As well as violins and violas he made two types of cello, one long and narrow in the style of Stradivari's 'Forma B' (see pp. 32-5), the other short and broad and generally more Amatisé. This cello, dated 1740, is of the latter type and is a beautiful example of preservation and craftsmanship. The arching has a full swell, which is not undermined by excessive scooping of the edges. However, there is some lack of thoroughness in the work; for example where the edge fluting meets the arching, there is a slight ridge where the contour remains unblended. The back, in particular, has traces of toothed plane and scraper marks. The purflings have been carefully inlaid, and the tidy mitres are short and undeflected. The soundholes are sharply cut, but no attempt has been made to sculpt the lower wings.

The head is cleanly carved and volutes of the scroll are deeply dished, not altogether characteristic of Celoniato, suggesting the hand of an assistant. The fluting channels around the head are also very deeply cut.

The choice of wood is unusual: the back and sides are of figured poplar, the head is of lime. The table has been made in three sections of pine, the centre piece of wide grain, and the flanks of a slightly closer growth. The attractive oil varnish which abundantly covers this instrument is of a pale golden-brown colour.

PRINCIPAL DIMENSIONS (mm)

Body

length	739	
upper bouts	360	
middle bouts	250	
lower bouts	440	

Rib Heights

neck root	119.5
upper corner	119.5
lower corner	120
end pin	121

Edge Thickness (back)

corners	5.2
centre	5.2
bouts	5

Stop Length   399

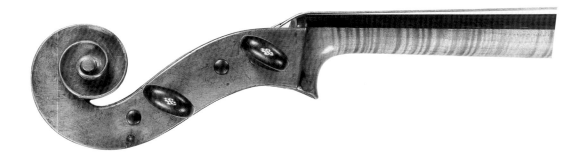

Joannes Francesco Pressenda: Turin

Violin 1833

Pressenda (1777-1854), along with his pupil Joseph Rocca, is regarded as the finest Italian maker of the nineteenth century. It is believed that he received training from the earlier Turin maker Alexandre d'Espine. Pressenda's style is modelled closely on Stradivari, but his instruments are not direct copies. The masculine outline is broader, the shoulders rounder and the arching fuller, particularly around the bridge area.

The 1833 violin is an example of the maker at his best, showing his keen eye for detail and his refined and capable craftsmanship. It is in remarkably fresh condition. The purflings are beautifully inlaid and the flutings deep and well defined. The well-sited soundholes are long and slender, becoming slightly pointed at the extremes. The broad, flamed maple of the back glows magnificently beneath a generous covering of luminous orange varnish; in areas where the top varnish has worn away the ground reflects light from dark yellow to a light cinnamon colour. The table is of a good-quality wide-grain spruce.

Looking at the head, the volutes are deeply carved and hollowed, with blackened edges in the manner of the Cremonese makers, and the deeply scored and clearly visible centre line between the flutings is a characteristic of the maker's work.

PRINCIPAL DIMENSIONS (mm)

Body			*Edge Thickness (back)*	
length	357		corners	4.2
upper bouts	168		centre	4
middle bouts	114		bouts	3.5
lower bouts	209			
			Stop Length	194
Rib Heights				
neck root	30			
upper corner	32			
lower corner	32			
end pin	32			

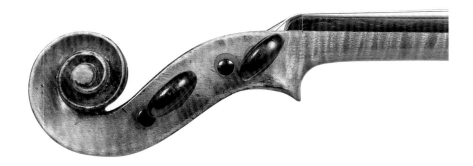

Joannes Francesco Pressenda: Turin
Violin 1847

In terms of workmanship and preservation there is much similarity between Pressenda's 1833 and 1847 violins. The later instrument is generally more compact and the bouts are slightly square-looking. The varnish is warm orange and of a thinner application.

Interestingly, the instrument still retains its original neck. In all the other instruments illustrated in this book, as with most violins, violas and cellos made before the mid-nineteenth century, the original neck and bass bar have been replaced to accommodate changes in string length, tension and playing technique: in this procedure the original head is retained and grafted onto a new neck. In this case the head and neck is carved from one piece of plain maple of a tight growth. The back and sides are of quarter-sawn maple of a light and attractive figure, and the table spruce is of a medium width.

PRINCIPAL DIMENSIONS (mm)

Body			*Edge Thickness (back)*	
length	355		corners	3.7
upper bouts	168		centre	3.5
middle bouts	112		bouts	3.4
lower bouts	206			
			Stop Length	194
Rib Heights				
neck root	30			
upper corner	31			
lower corner	31.6			
end pin	31.8			

69

APPENDICES
Bibliography and Discography

BIBLIOGRAPHY

J. Backus, *The Acoustical Foundations of Music*. Norton, New York 1969.

C. Beare, *Capolavori Di Antonio Stradivari*. Arnoldo Mondadori Editore, Milan 1987.

C. Bevan (Ed.), *Musical Instrument Collections in the British Isles*. Piccolo Press 1990.

C. Bonetti, *A Genealogy of the Amati Family of Violin Makers 1500-1740*, Trans. G.G. Champe. Maecenas Press 1989.

D. Boyden, *Catalogue of the Hill Collection of Musical Instruments in The Ashmolean Museum*. Oxford University Press 1969.

L.M. Condax, *Final Summary Report of Violin Varnish Research Project*. Mellon Institute No 3070, Pittsburgh 1970.

G. Hart, *The Violin: its Famous Makers and their Imitators*. Dulau & Co. 1875.

W. Henley, *Universal Dictionary of Violin and Bow Makers*. Amati Publishing 1973.

W.H., A.F. and A.E. Hill, *Antonio Stradivari, His Life and Work 1644-1737*. W.E. Hill & Sons 1902; and *The Violin Makers of the Guarneri Family*. W.E. Hill & Sons 1931.

M.L. Huggins, *Gio. Paolo Maggini, His Life and Work*. W.E. Hill & Sons 1892.

W. Monical, *Shapes of the Baroque*. American Federation of Violin and Bow Makers 1989.

S.F. Sacconi, *The Secrets of Stradivari*, Trans. A. Dipper. Libreria Del Convegno Cremona 1979.

S. Sadie (Ed.), *The New Grove Dictionary of Music & Musicians*. MacMillan 1990.

Count Cozio Di Salabue, *Carteggio*, Ed. G. Iriglia. Milan 1950; and English trans. of extracts by A. Dipper and D. Woodrow. Taynton, Oxon 1987.

W. Sandys and S.A. Forster, *The History of the Violin*. W. Reeves 1864.

DISCOGRAPHY

Amati Viola 1620, Paul Silverthorne:
Brahms - *Viola Sonatas, and Songs with Viola* (Meridian).

Amati Violin 1671 & **Dalla Costa Violin 1762**, Bingham Quartet:
Elizabeth Maconchy - *String Quartets Nos 5-8* (Unicorn/Kachana).
Haydn - *String Quartets Op. 33 Vol. 1, & Vol. 2* (CKCL).

Amati Violin c.1713, Chris Nicholls:
Bernard Van Dieren - *Sonata for Solo Violin Op. 5*, previously unrecorded (Whitetower).

Stradivari Violin 1694 'Rutson', Kenneth Sillito:
Vivaldi - *Four Seasons*, with Virtuoso of England Orchestra (Classics for Pleasure).
Bach - *Double Violin Concerto* with Hugh Bean, & *Violin Concerto in A Minor* (Classics for Pleasure).
Beethoven - *Quartets* Op. 18, 59, 74, 95 with Gabrielli Quartet (Decca).

Stradivari Viola 1696 'Archinto', Lindsay Quartet, Roger Bigley:
Beethoven/Bartók - *Complete Quartets*, with Peter Cropper playing the **Stradivari 1718 'Maurin'** (ASV).

Stradivari Violin 1699 'Kustendyke', Darlington Quartet, Colin Sauer:
Glazunov - *Two Quartets* (Pearl).

Stradivari Violin 1718 'Maurin', Alberni Quartet, Howard Davis:
Borodin - *Quartet No 2*
Tchaikovsky - *Quartets*.
Beethoven - *Late Quartets* (Collins Classics).

Mozart - *Quartets* (Pickwick).
Haydn - *Quartets*, Op. 76 (Collins Classics).

Stradivari Cello 1726 'Marquis de Corberon', Zara Nelsova:
Dvořák - *Cello Concerto & Rondo and Silent Woods* (MMC Vox).
Bloch - *Schelomo Rhapsody for Cello Solo and Orchestra* (Vauquard, Cardinal Series).
Beethoven - *Five Sonatas and Variations*, with Arthur Balsam (London Records).
Chopin, Rachmaninov, Franck, Poulenc - *Sonatas for Cello and Piano* (Golden Crest).
Hindemith - *Sonatas*, with Grant Johannesen, and with Grant Johannesen & Casadesus (Golden Crest).

Stradivari Violin 1734 'Habeneck', Ralph Holmes:
Delius - *Sonatas for Violin & Piano*, with Eric Fenby (Unicorn).
'Hommage to Kreisler' - *Violin & Piano Pieces*, with James Walker (Argo).
Prokofiev/Reger/Bartók - *Works for Solo Violin* (Argo).
Vivaldi - *Four Seasons*, with Cantilena (RCA).
Harty - *Violin Concerto*, with Ulster Orchestra (Chandos).
Sibelius - *Complete Smaller Works for Violin and Orchestra*, with Berlin Radio Symphony Orchestra (Schwann).
Beethoven - *Violin and Piano Sonatas*, with Richard Burnett (Amon).
Hummel - *Violin and Piano Sonatas*, with Richard Burnett (Amon).
Delius - *Violin Concerto*, Royal Philharmonic Orchestra (Unicorn/Kachana).

London Chamber Orchestra, Christopher Warren-Green: *LCO 1-10*, including:
Vaughan Williams - *The Lark Ascending*,
Mozart - *Violin Concerto No 5*,
Vivaldi - *Concerto for Two Violins in A minor*, with Rosemary Furniss playing the **Stradivari 1694 'Rutson'** (Virgin Classics).

Grancino Viola *c.*1690-1700, Alberni Quartet, John White:
Haydn - *String Quartets Nos 2 & 3*, Op. 33 (Saga).
Rawsthorne - *Complete Quartets* (Argo).
 Alberni Quartet, Berian Evans:
Mendelssohn - *Quartet in A minor*, & *Quartet in A Minor*.
Schubert - *Cello Quintet*.
Schumann - *Complete Quartets*.
 Maggini Quartet, Martin Outram:
Haydn - *String Quartets Nos 1, 2 & 5* Op. 33 (Pro Musica).

Guadagnini Violin *c.*1753, Alberni Quartet, Howard Davis:
Mendelssohn - *Quartet in A minor Op. 13.*

Schumann - *Three String Quartets*, & *Piano Quintet, Piano Quartet.*
Shostakovich - *Piano Quintet.*
Britten - *Three Quartets.*
Verdi/Puccini/Donizetti - *Quartets* (CRD).
Schubert - *Cello Quintet* (CRD).
Brahms - *Sextets (CRD).*
Granados - *Piano Quintet, Wordsworth Quartets* (CRD).

Guadagnini Violin *c.*1765, Alan Brind:
Sibelius - *Violin Concerto* (Chandos).

Pressenda Violin 1833, Jean Harvey:
Nielsen - *Unaccompanied violin works* (Chandos, originally BBC).

Pressenda Violin 1847, Hanson Quartet, Peter Hanson:
Elizabeth Maconchy - *String Quartets Nos 1-4* (Unicorn/Kachana).

Five of the Academy's Stradivaris with their holders in 1979:
Kenneth Sillito, 'Rutson'; Ralph Holmes, 'Habeneck'; Zara Nelsova, 'Marquis de Corberon'; Max Gilbert, 'Archinto'; Colin Sauer, 'Kustendyke'.

Glossary of Violin Making Terms

ARCHING The curved contours of the plates.

BACK The underside of the body.

BODY The soundbox, consisting of the front, back and ribs.

BODY STOP The distance from the edge of the table at the neck root to the bridge position.

BOUTS The six ribs form three main sections of the body: Upper bouts, or shoulders; the top section; Lower, or bottom bouts; the lower section; Middle bouts, or C bouts, the two concave ribs; the middle section.

CHANNELS The two lines of fluting which are carved around the head and down the back of the pegbox.

CHEEKS The side walls of the pegbox.

CORNERS The four points on the back and front where the upper and lower bouts meet the C bouts.

EDGES The border of the plate outside the purfling line.

EYE The small central circle of the volute.

FIGURE Flame or curl; in maple, the silvery light-reflecting patterns across the grain.

FLANKS The side parts of the arching.

FLUTING The hollowing of the edges above the purfling.

FORM The general modelling, and size.

FRONT Table or Belly, the upperside of the body.

GRAIN The wood fibres (growth lines) running the length of the plates.

HEAD The pegbox and scroll.

LININGS Reinforcing strips of wood which are glued to the upper and lower interior edges of the ribs. They serve to increase the gluing area between the ribs and the plates.

MAPLE A European hardwood, with several sub-species, generally used to make the back, sides and head.

MASTIC Resin obtained from the tree *Pistachia lentiscus*, used in varnish making. The word is used generally to describe various filling compounds.

MITRES The points where the purflings meet at the corners.

MOULD Used in making, a wooded structure around which the ribs are formed.

NICKS The notches in the soundhole, the inside nicks determine the position of the bridge.

OVERHANG Rounded border of the plates extending beyond the ribs.

PEGBOX The backward-curving and open-topped box which holds the four tuning pegs.

PLATES Back and/or Front.

PURFLING Normally, three narrow strips of wood, the two outer strips stained black, which are inlaid around the edge of the plates. The purflings serve as an ornamentation and to prevent the edge from splitting.

QUARTER-CUT Wood which is radially sawn or split with the grain.

SCRAPER Flat or curved blade which is used in finishing wood surfaces before varnishing.

SCROLL The spiralling ornamental part of the head.

SLAB-CUT Wood cut across the grain, in planks.

SOUNDHOLES The two 'f'-shaped openings on either side of the bridge.

SPRUCE/PINE Light-weight and resonant softwood, with several sub-species, used to make fronts.

STOP LENGTH See Body Stop.

TOOTHED IRON Plane with a toothed blade, used for working highly figured wood.

VOLUTE The spiralling turns of the scroll.

WINGS (SOUNDHOLE) The squared ends of the sound-holes contained within the upper and lower curves.